Forever Butterflies

Elizabeth Carrell

About the Book

Elizabeth chose to write about butterflies, because she has a love of butterflies since she was a child. What she did was do some researching about butterflies to help her audience learn more about butterflies. A few years ago, Elizabeth and her husband had the opportunity to go to Branson, MO. While there, the two discovered that there is a place to go see the butterflies. The butterflies are so beautiful that both Elizabeth and her husband took pictures. First thing the two did was watch a movie about butterflies. From there, the two went into a room with a controlled atmosphere along with a room that the people can see the metamorphosis of a butterfly. Elizabeth and her husband found this to be very educational. Butterflies are all over the world and very beautiful to look at.

Table of Content

1

Questions on Butterflies

Butterflies are beautiful. Here are some questions to think about. What is a butterfly? What is the life cycle of butterflies? What food do they eat? Who are their predators? Which butterflies fly long distance? Do people eat butterflies? What are the names of butterflies? Where is all the different variety of butterflies live? These and many more questions will be answered in the next few chapters.

WHAT IS A BUTTERFLY?

What is a butterfly? Butterflies are flying insects. They have large scaly wings with six jointed legs, three body parts, a pair antennae, eyes, and exoskeleton. The three body parts are the head, thorax (chest), and abdomen (tail end). Their bodies are covered with tiny sensory hairs. Each butterfly has four wings and six legs that are attached to thorax. The thorax has muscles which make the legs and wings move. All butterflies have different shapes, size, wing color, and wingspan. With this in mind, a person can tell the difference between a swallowtail to a longwings. There is a difference between the moth and a butterfly. The moth will stretch out its wings when not flying. As of the butterfly, the butterfly will spread its wings upward.

Butterflies are harmless insects. They don't bite, hurt anyone, or poisonous to kill anyone. Yet, they are beautiful to look at. To watch them to grow and develop into butterflies are fascinating. The butterflies can communicate by color, chemicals, sound, and physical action. When it rains, the butterflies hide under large leaves. Butterflies hide themselves by blending themselves when resting. They do this to make it harder for people and predators to find them.

All butterflies are good fliers. Each butterfly has veins that support the wings which feed blood. Butterflies can fly better with temperature above **60** degrees and they love to sun themselves. As each butterfly age, their colors fade. The fastest butterflies which is the Monarch

Butterfly can fly up to 20 miles per hour or faster. As for the slower butterflies, they fly five miles per hour. Butterflies migrate all over the world. The Painted Lady Butterfly, the red Admiral, and Common Buckeye travel a short distance due to cold weather. The Monarchs migrate thousands of miles. The next chapter is about the metamorphosis.

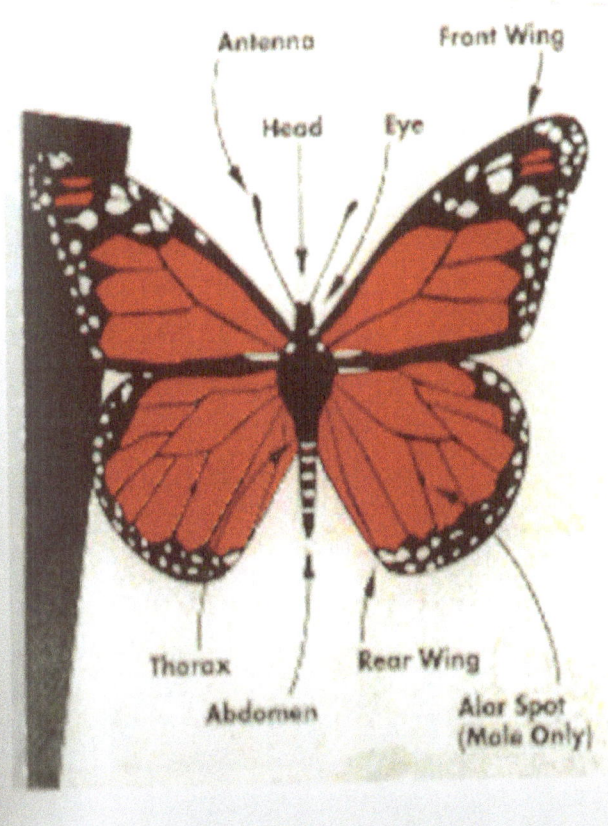

Antenna Front Wing

Head Eye

Thorax

Abdomen

Rear Wing

Alar Spot
(Male Only)

THE LIFE CYCLE OF A BUTTERFLY

The life of a butterfly is first, the egg, larva (caterpillar) pupa, and adult. How do butterflies mate and how long? Male and female butterflies linked themselves together for an hour or overnight just long enough for the sperm packet passes to the female.

First, the female will lay her eggs on the leaves. The eggs will take about ten days to hatch. Second, the eggs hatch into caterpillars.

Caterpillars will first eat their shells, leaves, and some other caterpillars. The caterpillars are brightly colored and will camouflage themselves to the shade that will match the plants. This is their way of not being seen by their predators. Some caterpillars may have eye-like markings on their body to scare predators and sheds their skins as they grow. Their hiding places are in the leaves. Some caterpillars live among the ants due to the sweet liquid that the ants love. In order to help the caterpillars, the ants will drive the predators away. Third, after the caterpillars are fully grown, they look for a suitable place to start their pupa stage. Last, it may weeks or months for the transformation of a butterfly.

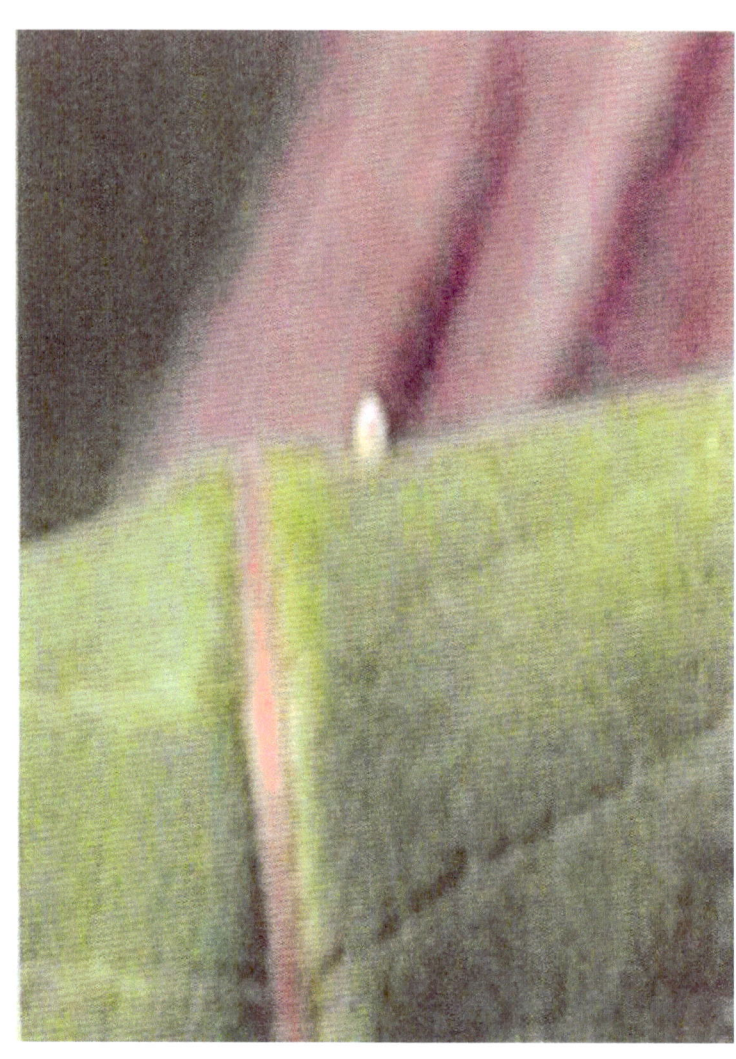

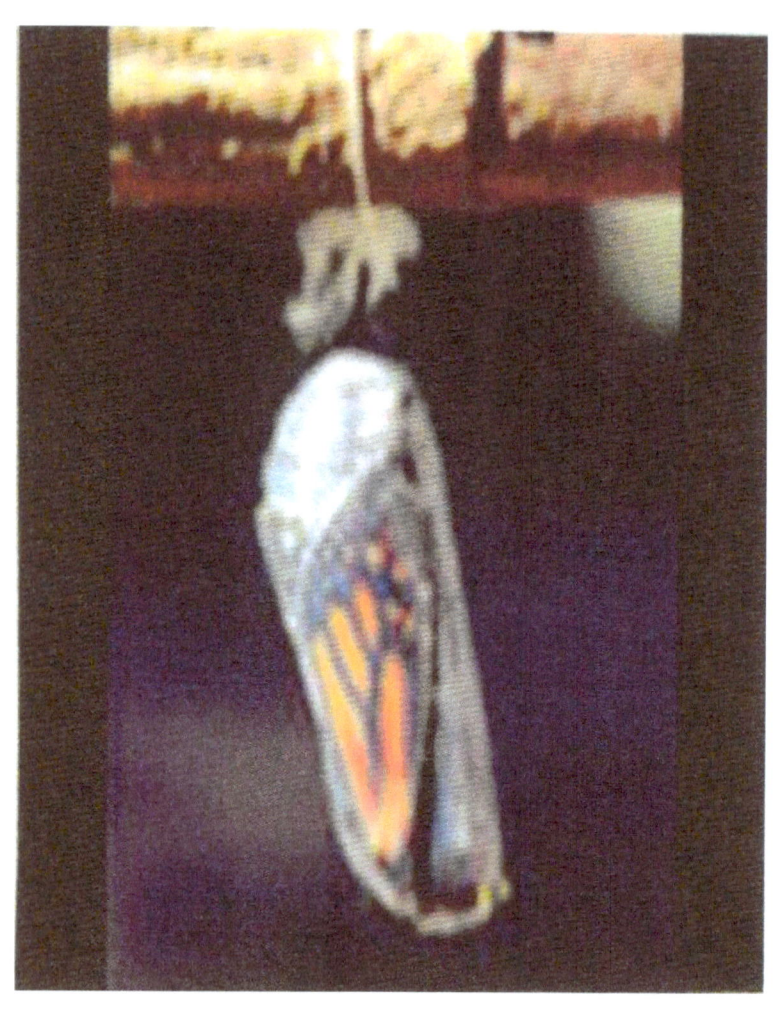

Their Predators

Butterflies do have predators. For example, when a bird eats a butterfly, the bird will get sick by vomiting and remember not to eat butterflies of that kind. Not to worry, the birds will not die. Monarch Butterflies have a bad taste due to the caterpillars eating the milkweed. The Viceroy will not be touched by birds due to the fact that the butterfly looks like a Monarch Butterfly.

There are two types of mimicry. The first is the batesian and the second one is the mullerian. The mimicry butterflies are a batesian mimicry. They are non-poisonous even though they have the same markings as poisonous butterflies. The markings give these butterflies protection.

Now the Mullerian mimicry is poisonous butterflies with similar markings as the Batesian mimicry. These butterflies are the swallowtails. Other predators are praying mantis, wasps, ants, parasites flies, snakes, toads, rats, lizards, dragonflies, and monkeys. People in Mexico, Africa, and Southeast Asia will eat butterflies for dessert.

VARIETIES OF BUTTERFLIES

There are many varieties of butterflies. Let's take a look at the Monarch Butterfly. The final generation of the Monarch Butterflies comes out of hibernation in February and March. First, the butterflies find a mate. Then, they migrate to the North and East to lay their eggs on milkweed plants. The metamorphosis begins. It takes four days for the eggs to hatch. The caterpillars are fully grown in just two weeks. Then, they are in a cocoon for ten days. Once the butterflies are formed, they feed on flowers and die in about two to six weeks after laying their eggs.

The second generation is born in May and June. In July and August, the third generation is born. As for the fourth generation (born September and October), the butterflies do not die. Instead, they migrate to California and Mexico. The butterflies live there for six to eight months and the process starts over again.

Next butterfly to talk about is the Pipevine Swallowtail. The Pipevine Swallowtail has a shiny blue body with white spots on upper side of hind wings and blue underneath. As for the hind wings, they are blue with one row of orange colors. This swallowtail fly closer to the ground and goes to a flower for a short time. The swallowtail butterflies love wooded areas and forest end.

The Orange Sulphur Butterfly is most hardy during the winter time. As for the Clouded Sulphurs and Cabbage Whites cannot survive the freezing weather. The

Lycaenidae Butterflies have blues, coppers, hairstreaks, and harvesters in color. Indeed, the butterflies have the metallic sheen. The males have short forelegs with no claws and the females have normal legs. The caterpillars look more like slugs.

Next to discuss is the Swamp Metalmark. These butterflies are small with rusty orange-brown and dime-sized for a wing span. The butterflies eat mountain mint, black-eyed Susan, swamp milkweed, shrubby cinquefoil, and yarrow.

The Lange's Metalmark Butterflies are bright colored butterfly. They are from the Riodinidae family and a small butterfly. Their wingspan is one to 1.5 inches with black along with white spots and red-orange on the inner half of the forewing. The hindwing base is black and the wings are gray, white, black, and orange. What the butterflies eat are buckwheat, butterweed, and snakeweed. There is only one generation a year for these butterflies.

Next is the Red-spotted Purple Family. These butterflies are blue iridescent wings with orange spots underside. They mimic the Pipevine Swallowtail and from the brush-footed family. The place the butterflies are to the wooded areas and edges. They like overripe fruit.

The Mardon Skipper Butterfly is small and tawny-orange. The butterflies have a hairy body. Upper wings are orange with dark borders. Lower wings are light tan-orange with light yellow and white spots. The reason these butterflies have the skipper name are their fast skipping flight. These skippers are found in prairie and meadow and abundant in Idaho. The adult skippers love a variety plants, but their favorite are the blue violets.

Next to discuss is the Silver-spotted Skipper which is one of the skipper butterflies. These butterflies feed at night. The Long-tailed Skipper looks like a swallowtail. The butterflies expand to two inches and dark brown with silvery spots on each front wing.

The Juvenal's Dusky-wing attacks oak trees. Birds, spiders, predaceous beetles, and other enemies that the caterpillars need shelter from. These caterpillars have to stay out of rain and snow. If they get wet, the caterpillars will die from the freezing weather. Other skippers are Sooty Wing, Smaller Skippers, Roadside Skipper, and Least Skipper.

6

THE DIFFERENT VARIETY OF
BUTTERFLIES LIVE IN THE WORLD

One of the questions, where does all the different variety of butterflies live is all over the world. Some like the Monarch migrate. Swamp Metalmark live in Wisconsin. Lang's Metalmark lives in San Francisco, California. Brushfoot Butterflies also live in Wisconsin. Mardon Skipper Butterflies live in Idaho, Oregon, and Washington. Giant Skippers live in the southwestern states, Mexico, Colorado, and Florida. The Long-tailed Skippers are found along the Gulf Coast from Mexico to Florida. They live along the Atlantic Coast to New York City and to Connecticut, but very rare. The Juvenal's

Dusky-wing Butterfly is found from New Hampshire to the Great Plains and south to the Gulf of Mexico. Next is the Persius's Dusky-wing Butterfly. These butterflies live from coast to coast. They live in the Eastern states, Florida, and along the Pacific Coast. The first set of the smaller skipper butterflies are the Tawny-edged Skipper Butterflies. These butterflies can be found in Nova Scotia, British Columbia, the Rocky Mountains, New Mexico, Texas, and Florida. The Roadside Skipper Butterfly lives mostly in the United States. Here is a list of some of the butterflies in the world.

North American Butterflies:

Parnassians and Swallowtails:

Clodius Parnassian

Rocky Mountain Parnassian

Pipevine Swallowtail

Polydamas Swallowtail

Zebra Swallowtail

Black Swallowtail

Anise Swallowtail

Giant Swallowtail

Eastern Tiger Swallowtail

Appalachian tiger Swallowtail

Canadian Tiger Swallowtail

Western Tiger Swallowtail

Two-Tailed Swallowtail

Pale Swallowtail

Spicebush Swallowtail

Palamedes Swallowtail

Whites and Sulpurs:

Pine White

Florida White

Checkered White

Western White

Cabbage White

Great Southern White

Large Marble

Stella Orangetip

Queen Alexandra's Sulphur

Sierra Sulphur

Cloudless Sulphur

Large Orange Sulphur

California Dogface

Barred Yellow

Mexican Yellow

Mimosa Yellow

Dainty Sulphur

Harvesters, Coppers, Hairstreaks, and Blues:

Harvester

Great Copper

Ruddy Copper

Purplish Copper

Red-Banded Hairstreak

Marine Blue

Miami Blue

Melissa Blue

Little Metalmark

Mormon Metalmark

Palmer's Metalmark

Brushfoots:

American Snout

Mormon Fritillary

Gorgone Checkerspot

Tiny Checkerspot

Cuban Crescent

Pearl Crescent

Mylitta Crescent

Edith's Checkerspot

American Lady

Painted Lady

West Coast Lady

California Sister

Common Ringlet

Monarch

Queen

Soldier

Skippers:

Mangrove Skipper

Silver-Spotted Skipper

Acacia Skipper

Mournful Duskywing

Green Skipper

Indian Skipper

Nevada Skipper

Purple-washed Skipper

Mexican butterflies:

Archaic Swallowtail

Pipevine Swallowtail

Polydamas Swallowtail

Colima Swallowtail

Yellow-trailed Swallowtail

Confused Swallowtail

Yellow-trailed Swallowtail

White-dotted Cattleheart

Pink-spotted Cattleheart

Montezuma's Cattleheart

Pink-Checked Cattleheart

Green-celled Cattleheart

Emerald-patched Cattleheart

Wedge-spotted Cattleheart

Transandean Cattleheart

Guatemalan Kite-Swallowtail

Bow-lined Kite Swallowtail

Thick-bordered Kite-Swallowtail

Yellow Kite-Swallowtail

Orange Kite-Swallowtail

Salvin's Kite-Swallowtail

White-crescent Swallowtail

Dual-spotted Swallowtail

Red-sided Swallowtail

Black Swallowtail

Band-gapped Swallowtail

Giant Swallowtail

Thoas Swallowtail

Ornythion Swallowtail

Broad-banded Swallowtail

Androgeus Swallowtail

Magnificent Swallowtail

Oaxacan Swallowtail

Two-tailed Swallowtail

Eastern Tiger Swallowtail

Pamamedes Swallowtail

Three-tailed Swallowtail

Ruby-spotted Swallowtail

Pink-spotted Swallowtail

Yucatan Swallowtail

Pale-spotted Swallowtail

Victorine Swallowtail

Western Pygmy-Blue

Cassius Blue

Marine Blue

Cyna Blue

Ceraunus Blue

Reakirt's Blue

Eastern Tailed-Blue

Spring Azure

Acmon Blue

Lilac-bottomed Sombermark

Golden Sombermark

Purple-topped Sombermark

Transistional Sombermark

Mystical Sombermark

Orange-costa Sombermark

Red-rayed Sombermark

Inconspicuous Sombermark

Pearly Sombermark

Orange-angled Sombermark

Brown-and-gray Sombermark

Brown-posted Sombermark

Fiery Sombermark

Orange-flushed Eyemark

Purple-washed Eyemark

Turquoise Eyemark

Blue-winged Sheenmark

Sonoran Metalmark

Quilted Metalmark

Orchid Metalmark

Cherry-bordered Metalmark

Blue-and-yellow Beautymark

Two-oranges Metalmark

Red-bordered Metalmark

Hackberry Greenmark

Red-spotted Greenmark

Blue Metalmark

Mormon Metalmark

Palmer's Metalmark

Murphy's Metalmark

Persian Metalmark

Hepburn's Metalmark

Walker's Metalmark

Crescent Metalmark

Hackberry Emperor

Tawny Emperor

Cyan Emperor

Turquoise Emperor

Monarch

Queen

Soldier

Tiger Mimic-Queen

Cloud-forest Monarch

Golden Banded-Skipper

Sierra Madre Banded-Skipper

Sonoran Banded-Skipper

Chisos Banded-Skipper

Mimosa Skipper

Acacia Skipper

Gold-costa Skipper

Purplish-black Skipper

Golden-headed Scallopwing

Mazans Scallopwing

Aztec Scallopwing

Variegated Skipper

Blue-studded Skipper

Royal Spurwing

Texas Powdered-Skipper

Arizona Powdered-Skipper

False Duskywing

Four-spotted Skipperling

Violet-patched Skipper

Clouded Skipper

Green-backed Ruby-eye

Sunrise Skipper

Morrison's Skipper

Apache Skipper

Green Skipper

Glowing Skipper

Moon-marked Skipper

Violet=clouded Skipper

Brazilian Skipper

British Isles:

Peacock

Adonis Blue

Orange Tip

New Hampshire Species of butterflies do include the American Copper, Coral Hairstreak, Eastern Tailed-Blue, Frosted Elfin, and Karner Blue Butterfly. Other countries that have butterflies are Europe, Amazon and the Andes, Africa, Asia, India, Malaysia and Borneo, New Guinea, Australia, and New Zealand. There are about 28,000 species of butterflies all over the world.

7

BUTTERFLY GARDEN

As mention from a previous chapter, butterflies the sun. Some people like to do a butterfly garden outside their home. Butterfly feeders, a flat stone for butterflies can rest, and a mud puddle is some of the ways to attract butterflies. Here is a list of some of the plants that attract butterflies.

List of Nectar Plants:

Flowers:

Aster

Black-Eyed Susan

Blazing Stars

Butterfly Milkweed

Buttonbush

Cardinal Flower

Common Milkweed

Coneflowers

Coreopsis

Dianthus Family

False Nettle

Hollyhock

Indian Paintbrush

Lantana

Mallow

Marigold

Mexican Sunflowers

Nasturtium

Petunia

Pussy-toe

Rue

Ruellia

Salvia

Shasta Daisy

Silver Brocade

Snapdragon

Spider flower

Sunflower

Swamp Milkweed

Swamp Verbena

Tall Verbena

Thistle

Violet

Water Dock

Wild Senna

Woodland Stonecrop

Yarrow

Zinnias

Herbs:

Dill

Fennel

Parsley

Grasses:

Little Bluestem Grass

Orchard Grass

Panic Grass

Shrubs:

Butterfly Bush

Coontie

False Indigo

Spicebush

Vines:

Passion Flowers

Pipevine

Trees:

Aspen tree

Chaste Tree

Common HopTree

Elm Tree

Flowering Dogwood

Pawpaw

Prickly Ash

Sassafras

Sweet Bay

Willow

To put on the ground:

Overripe fruit

Bananas

Oranges

Pears

Raising butterflies in the homes are great in teaching the children about butterflies. Some of the butterflies that are great to attract are the Anise Swallowtail and the

Black Swallowtail. If the eggs are laid on a potted plant

can be brought indoors to watch the caterpillars come out

of the eggs. The caterpillars when touched may give out

an unpleasant like rotten cheese or foul.

8

PLACES TO VISIT BUTTERFLIES

As stated in chapter six that there are butterflies all over the world. In this chapter will be places where one can go see the butterflies free from other predators. Here is the list of places to see the butterflies in the United States and other countries.

United States:

Tucson, Arizona

Gainesville, Florida

Navarre, Florida

New Orleans, Louisiana

Branson, Missouri

Springfield, Missouri

Lincoln, Nebraska

Durham, North Carolina

Cincinnati, Ohio

Dallas, Texas

Milwaukee, Wisconsin

Other countries:

Kuronda, Australia

Queensland, Australia

Belize- two locations

Canada:

Coombs, British Columbia

Niagara Falls, Ontario

Sudbury, Ontario

Victoria, Canada

Cambridge, Ontario

Central America-Hunduras-one location

Costa Rica-three locations

Phillippines-one location

United Kingdom:

Wales

DIFFERENCE BETWEEN MALE AND FEMALE BUTTERFLIES

It is hard to believe that there would a difference between male and female butterflies. The only ones that are noticeable would be the birds. Like the male birds, the male butterflies have the bright colors. Same way as the female bird, the female butterflies have lots of brown.

The behavior of the male butterflies is perched, in control, and search for females. As for the female butterflies, they search for plants to lay their eggs. Another interesting note is that some caterpillars have more legs than others.

THE CONCLUSION

In the previous chapters that were discussed about butterflies, they are harmless insects. Yet, they are beautiful to watch them fly from flower to flower. The butterflies do not kill anyone nor hurt them.

Chapter one had many questions. The first one is about the life cycle of butterflies. Watching the metamorphosis of a butterfly is very fascinating and to think that anyone can watch it happen in his or her yard or in his or her home.

The next question that was answered was the food that butterflies eat. It is not hard to find the food for butterflies. Knowing who their predators are is very important. It is hard to believe that people from other countries eat butterflies as an appetizer. In chapter two stated which butterfly flies the fastest. It is interesting how a butterfly can communicate with other butterflies. Monarch Butterflies do fly the longest distance. There are so many names of butterflies in the entire world. Yes, it is true, butterflies are beautiful.

About the Author

Elizabeth Carrell was born and raised in Massachusetts and did not know how important education is until after she got married. After she got her high school diploma, she decided to get her college education. Although, Elizabeth did not finish her college education, she discovered that she can write an essay for her assignments and get a good grade. She decided to write stories about her cats. Her customers loved her stories that she decided to write a story about her dog.

www.ingramcontent.com/pod-product-compliance
Lightning Source LLC
Chambersburg PA
CBHW050751290526
45792CB00008B/2133